PLEASED TO SEE ME

I want

to do with you what spring does with the cherry trees.

PABLO NERUDA

Pleased to See Me

69

VERY SEXY POEMS

a cheeky number whipped up by

NEIL ASTLEY

BLOODAXE BOOKS

ISBN: 1 85224 614 6

First published 2002 by
Bloodaxe Books Ltd,
Highgreen,
Tarset,
Northumberland NE48 1RP.

www.bloodaxebooks.com
For further information about Bloodaxe titles
please visit our website or write to
the above address for a catalogue.

 Bloodaxe Books Ltd acknowledges
the financial assistance of Northern Arts.

Printed in Great Britain by
Cromwell Press Ltd, Trowbridge, Wiltshire.

Contents

[6]

Foreplay

NEIL ASTLEY

Poets have always written about sex. The tradition of bawdy, satirical and playful poetry about sex goes back to the Greeks and Romans, running through English poetry from Chaucer through Shakespeare to Herrick and Rochester before going underground for two centuries. Catullus and Martial wrote scathingly rude satires – much imitated by later poets – which were as much about hypocrisy and morals in privileged Roman society as about sex.

Often poets have been punished for their candour, or had their work banned or bowdlerised, or were forced into silence or self-censorship. The great Latin love poet Ovid, whose work profoundly influenced later European art and literature, was exiled for life by Emperor Augustus. In 1599, Christopher Marlowe's translations of Ovid were burned by order of the Church of England. In 1857, Charles Baudelaire was arrested and fined for publishing *Les Fleurs du Mal*, and six poems from this classic of French literature remained banned until 1949. A scholarly edition of Rochester's poetry was destroyed by the New York authorities in 1926, while the BBC had to make a public apology in 1934 for publishing Dylan Thomas's now inoffensive poem 'Light breaks where no sun shines'.

The tide finally turned with 'the end of the *Chatterley* ban' in 1960, but it took another 20 years before poets fully embraced a new imaginative freedom in writing about sex with honesty, passion and a boldly playful sense of humour. In the new celebratory 'writing from the body', the muse was no longer the woman as sex object. Euphemism – that sly cloak of erotic verse – was largely discarded; poems in this book by E.E. Cummings (*page 23*) and Robert Frost (*27*) are earlier examples of metaphorical sensuality at its crafty best.

Yeats called poetry 'truth seen with passion'. Contemporary poetry about sex is about passion seen with truth, about making love with language. 'Every new poem is like finding a new bride,' said American poet Stanley Kunitz. 'Words are so erotic, they never tire of their coupling.' The poems in *Pleased to See Me* are very sexy poems not just because they are about sex, but because their luscious language is handled with wit and sureness of touch. This is the first book to show how the way poets write about sex has changed dramatically. As in so much else, the boundaries have shifted. Sex in modern poetry – as in films, novels and music – is treated freely and frankly, with passion, tenderness and a great sense of fun. Expect surprises and reversals as well as creepiness and unease, coupled with in-your-face exuberance. We're talking strong language and strong emotion here.

And the women are calling the shots. The most forthright and unashamedly confident poet writing about sex is America's Sharon Olds. Nearly two-thirds of the poems in this selection are by women, in contrast with earlier compilations, such as *Making Love: The Picador Book of Erotic Verse* (1978), edited by Alan Bold, who claimed it was 'true of erotic poetry, as of poetry generally, that most of the practitioners are male' to justify a selection of less than 5% women. John Whitworth's *Faber Book of Blue Verse* (1990) had less than 15%.

It's not only the dominant gender that has shifted, but the way the poets write about both gender and sex. Claudia Rankine's description of how Katy Lederer's poems 'reinvent the language of love, denuding historically predetermined scripts' could apply to many other poets here, as in Vicki Feaver's response (*25*) to a nude by Roger Hilton: 'As a woman I ought to object. / But she looks happy enough.' Deryn Rees-Jones takes the lead in 'Lovesong to Captain James T. Kirk' (*76*), straddling her *Star Trek* hero. Guyanan Grace Nichols' poems about sex (*18*) are fired by postcolonial assertiveness. The classic bawdy male tradition carries on in brilliant comic verse by writers such as Gavin Ewart, Brendan Kennelly and Whitworth himself, but that is not the vein of poetry covered by this book.

Linda France wrote of her Bloodaxe anthology *Sixty Women Poets* (1993): 'The poetry has a wild quality, the sense of a creature constrained too long, wanting to taste earthy pleasures, untrammelled by the still cautious eyes of a culture fuelled by guilt and containment.'

That is also true of the celebratory, sensual, passionate and playful poems about sex – by men as well as women – in *Pleased to See Me*.

Modern poetry about sex often involves the reinvention of roles and literary models. Basil Bunting's 'O, it is godlike to sit self-possessed' (*61*) is a tribute to Catullus (the Latin epigraph is his opening line), whose first stanza in the Latin is itself a translation from a Greek poem by Sappho. Bunting's version triumphantly recasts the whole poem in his own reinvented Sapphic stanzas so freshly that the poem reads not as a translation but as a new-minted English poem directly addressed to an obliging lover. Linda France's 'The Feckless Gypsy' (*66*) – from a sequence of poems called *On the Game* – changes Lorca's Spanish gypsy lover of a faithless wife to a prostitute toying with a despised married client. Jo Shapcott sees the roses in Rilke's French poems as women, translating them into female genitalia with a voice of their own (*19*). Sarah Maguire, a powerful chronicler of the dispossessed, meditates on a sexual encounter while working on a feminist history in her poem 'Spilt Milk' (*65*). The Australian Dorothy Porter writes sensuous verse novels; her 'First Move' (*33*) begins a seduction sequence in *The Monkey's Mask* between her lesbian detective Jill and the book's *femme fatale*. Carol Ann Duffy remakes a poem of male homosexual love by Paul Verlaine into her 'Girlfriends' (*70*), while Craig Raine's 'Arsehole' (*22*) turns a notorious sonnet jointly written by Verlaine (the first eight lines) with Rimbaud (the last six) into a tender evocation of anal lovemaking between man and (probably) woman.

All the poems in this book have previously appeared in books and magazines from reputable imprints in Britain and America, including mainstream publishers, university presses and publicly-funded specialist poetry houses. But this is the first time, to my knowledge, that a selection of this nature and quality has been brought together in one anthology. I hope it comes as a revelation to all lovers of language.

First Sex

SHARON OLDS

I knew little, and what I knew
I did not believe – they had lied to me
so many times, so I just took it as it
came, his naked body on the sheet,
the tiny hairs curling on his legs like
fine, gold shells, his sex
harder and harder under my palm
and yet not hard as a rock his face cocked
back as if in terror, the sweat
jumping out of his pores like sudden
trails from the tiny snails when his knees
locked with little clicks and under my
hand he gathered and shook and the actual
flood like milk came out of his body, I
saw it glow on his belly, all they had
said and more, I rubbed it into my
hands like lotion, I signed on for the duration.

The Heavy Petting Zoo

CLARE POLLARD

It's your best friend's 16th birthday party.
That's eight hamster lives, and yet she still wasn't wise enough
to realise it would turn into a heavy-petting zoo.
Let's put it this way – you wouldn't bring the family,
and there's an awful lot of stroking going on.

The lounge crawls with muzzy, fuzzy pubic mice.
You want to hibernate, but every bedroom is locked.
(That soft-haired girl from the Shetlands is offering rides.)

You could have been a part of it –
for a small price at the door you could have had them
eating out of your hand by now,
felt that breathy, hot nuzzle-lick,
but instead you're floundering in your own sour
vinegar juices, like a sick terrapin.

The other girls are beautiful and brittle chicks,
eggs precarious and smashable in the cups of their bras,
and he's with her somewhere.

They're probably mewling cutely at each other,
or else she's stripped and pink as a piglet
and they're at it like rabbits.
It's sickeningly bestial.
You hope they get myxomatosis.

Yet in your small child's heart you know
that if he'd called you, you'd have followed him as she did.

As a lamb does, whitely and without question.

The
Bathing Girls

TRACEY HERD

Lighting her thin French cigarette
with a flaring match, flinging her head
back to exhale her looping signature
in smoke, she plucked April's *Vogue*
from her smart red corduroy satchel.

She wet her thumb and peeled
the cover back. Sunlight fell
on an interior pungent and dazzling
as freshly painted walls. I breathed
deeply and took the plunge.

Six bathing girls in strapless suits
linked arms and ran out from a cerulean
ocean, their ankles fluted columns
tilting through the waves.
I hugged my school books close

not wanting to see how my friend's sweater
clung to her tiny breasts, but unable
to take my eyes from her slicked red mouth.
I wanted to lean forward and kiss her.
In those days, anything seemed possible.

The Little Black Book

PAUL MULDOON

It was Aisling who first soft-talked my penis-tip between her legs
while teasing open that Velcro strip between her legs.

Cliona, then. A skinny country girl.
The small stream, in which I would skinny-dip, between her legs.

Born and bred in Londinium, the stand-offish Etain,
who kept a stiff upper lip between her legs.

Grainne. Grain goddess. The last, triangular shock of corn,
through which a sickle might rip, between her legs.

Again and again that winter I made a bee-line for Ita,
for the sugar-water sip between her legs.

The spring brought not only Liadan but her memory of Cuirithir,
his ghostly one-up-manship between her legs.

(Ita is not to be confused with her steely half-sister, Niamh,
she of the ferruginous drip between her legs.)

It was Niamh, as luck would have it, who introduced me to Orla.
The lost weekend of a day trip between *her* legs.

It was Orla, as luck would have it, who introduced me to Roisin.
The bramble-patch. The rosehip between her legs.

What ever became of Sile?
Sile who led me to horse-worship between her legs.

As for Janet from the Shankill, who sometimes went by 'Sinead',
I practised my double back-flip between her legs.

I had a one-on-one tutorial with Siobhan.
I read *The Singapore Grip* between her legs.

And what ever became of Sorcha, Sorcha, Sorcha?
Her weakness for the whip between her legs.

Or the big-boned, broad-shouldered Treasa?
She asked me to give her a buzzclip between her legs.

Or the little black sheep, Una, who kept her own little black book?
I fluttered, like an erratum slip, between her legs.

Early Images of Heaven

SHARON OLDS

It amazed me that the shapes of penises,
their sizes, and angles, everything about them
was the way I would have designed them if I had
invented them. The skin, the way the skin
thickens and thins, its suppleness,
the way the head barely fits in the throat,
its mouth almost touching the valve of the stomach –
and the hair, which lifts, or crinkles, delicate
and free – I could not get over all this,
the passion for it as intense in me
as if it were made to my order, or my
desire made to its order – as if I had
known it before I was born, as if
I remembered coming through it, like God
the Father all around me.

Balls

ANNE McNAUGHTON

Actually: it's the balls I look for, always.
Men in the street, offices, cars, restaurants.
It's the nuts I imagine –
firm, soft, in hairy sacks
the way they are
down there rigged between the thighs,
the funny way they are.
One in front, a little in front of the other,
slightly higher. The way they slip
between your fingers, the way they
slip around in their soft sack.
The way they swing when he walks,
hang down when he bends
over. You see them sometimes bright pink
out of a pair of shorts
when he sits wide and unaware,
the hair sparse and wiry
like that on a poland china pig.
You can see the skin right through – speckled,
with wrinkles like a prune, but loose,
slipping over those kernels
rocking the smooth, small huevos.
So delicate, the cock becomes a diversion,
a masthead overlarge, its flag distracting
from beautiful pebbles beneath.

My Black Triangle

GRACE NICHOLS

My black triangle
sandwiched between the geography of my thighs

is a bermuda
of tiny atoms
forever seizing
and releasing
the world

My black triangle
is so rich
that it flows over
on to the dry crotch
of the world

My black triangle
is black light
sitting on the threshold of the world
overlooking
all my deep probabilities

And though
it spares a thought for history
my black triangle
has spread beyond his story
beyond the dry fears of parch-ri-archy

Spreading and growing
trusting and flowing
my black triangle
carries the seal of approval
of my deepest self.

The Roses

(versions of Rilke's
French poems)

JO SHAPCOTT

Rosa foetida

I'm an imperfect thing:
neat, layered
but spilling petals and pollen,
dropping bruised scent

on to the ground.
Essence of roses is not sweet,
but brown at the edges
like the air you breathe.

Rosa pimpinellifolia

O I'm leaning
against your forehead,
against your eyelid,
scenting your skin

with my own,
making you think
you can sleep
inside my face.

Rosa odorata

I can't turn a smell
into a single word;
you've no right
to ask. Warmth
coaxes rose fragrance
from the underside of petals.

The oils meet air:
rhodinol is old rose;
geraniol, like geranium;
nerol is my essence
of magnolia; eugenol,
a touch of cloves.

Breasts

**MAXINE
CHERNOFF**

If I were French, I'd write
about breasts, structuralist treatments
of breasts, deconstructionist breasts,
Gertrude Stein's breasts in Père-Lachaise
under stately marble. Film noir breasts
no larger than olives, Edith Piaf's breasts
shadowed under a song, mad breasts raving
in the bird market on Sunday.
Tanguy breasts softening the landscape,
the politics of nipples (we're all equal).

A friend remembers nursing,
his twin a menacing blur. But wait,
we're in America, where breasts
were pointy until 1968. I once invented
a Busby Berkeley musical with naked women
underwater sitting at a counter
where David Bowie soda-jerked them
ice cream glaciers. It sounds so sexual
but had a Platonic airbrushed air.
Beckett calls them dugs, which makes me think
of potatoes, but who calls breasts potatoes?
Bolshoi dancers strap down their breasts
while practicing at the bar.
You guess they're thinking of sailing,
but probably it's bread, dinner,
and the *Igor Zlotik Show* (their
Phil Donahue). There's a photo of me
getting dressed where I'm surprised
by Paul and try to hide my breasts, and another
this year, posed on a pier, with my breasts
reflected in silver sunglasses. I blame
it on summer when flowers overcome gardens
and breasts point at the stars. Cats
have eight of them, and Colette tells
of a cat nursing its young while
being nursed by its mother. Imagine the scene
rendered human. And then there's the Russian
story about the woman...but wait,
they've turned the lights down, and Humphrey
Bogart is staring at Lauren Bacall's breasts
as if they might start speaking.

Arsehole

*(version of a sonnet
by Paul Verlaine
& Arthur Rimbaud)*

CRAIG RAINE

It is shy as a gathered eyelet
neatly worked in shrinking violet;
it is the dilating iris, tucked
away, a tightening throb when fucked.

It is a soiled and puckered hem,
the golden treasury's privy purse.
With all the colours of a bruise,
it is the fleck of blood in albumen.

I dreamed your body was an instrument
and this was the worn mouthpiece
to which my breathing lips were bent.

Each note pleaded to love a little longer,
longer, as though it was dying of hunger.
I fed that famished mouth my ambergris.

'she being Brand'

E.E. CUMMINGS

she being Brand

-new;and you
know consequently a
little stiff i was
careful of her and(having

thoroughly oiled the universal
joint tested my gas felt of
her radiator made sure her springs were O.

K.)i went right to it flooded-the-carburetor cranked her

up,slipped the
clutch(and then somehow got into reverse she
kicked what
the hell)next
minute i was back in neutral tried and

again slo-wly;bare,ly nudg.   ing(my

lev-er Right-
oh and her gears being in
A 1 shape passed
from low through
second-in-to-high like
greasedlightning)just as we turned the corner of Divinity

avenue i touched the accelerator and give

her the juice,good

                    (it

was the first ride and believe i we was
happy to see how nice she acted right up to
the last minute coming back down by the Public
Gardens i slammed on

the
internalexpanding
&
externalcontracting
brakes Bothatonce and

brought allofher tremB
-ling
to a:dead.

stand-
;Still)

Oi Yoi Yoi

(for Roger Hilton)

VICKI FEAVER

The lady has no shame.
Wearing not a stitch
she is lolloping across
an abstract beach
towards a notional sea.

I like the whisker of hair
under her armpit. It suggests
that she's not one of those women
who are always trying to get rid
of their smell.

You were more interested
in her swinging baroque tits
and the space between her thighs
than the expression on her face.
That you've left blank.

But her *mons veneris*
you've etched in black ink
with the exuberance of a young lad
caught short on a bellyful of beer
scrawling on a wall in the Gents.

As a woman I ought to object.
But she looks happy enough.
And which of us doesn't occasionally
want one of the old gods to come down
and chase us over the sands?

Rite of Spring

SEAMUS HEANEY

So winter closed its fist
And got it stuck in the pump.
The plunger froze up a lump

In its throat, ice founding itself
Upon iron. The handle
Paralysed at an angle.

Then the twisting of wheat straw
Into ropes, lapping them tight
Round stem and snout, then a light

That sent the pump up in flame.
It cooled, we lifted her latch,
Her entrance was wet, and she came.

The
Silken Tent

ROBERT FROST

She is as in a field a silken tent
At midday when a sunny summer breeze
Has dried the dew and all its ropes relent,
So that in guys it gently sways at ease,
And its supporting central cedar pole,
That is its pinnacle to heavenward
And signifies the sureness of the soul,
Seems to owe naught to any single cord,
But strictly held by none, is loosely bound
By countless silken ties of love and thought
To everything on earth the compass round,
And only by one's going slightly taut
In the capriciousness of summer air
Is of the slightest bondage made aware.

Taking Off Emily Dickinson's Clothes

BILLY COLLINS

First, her tippet made of tulle,
easily lifted off her shoulders and laid
on the back of a wooden chair.

And her bonnet,
the bow undone with a light forward pull.

Then the long white dress, a more
complicated matter with mother-of-pearl
buttons down the back,
so tiny and numerous that it takes forever
before my hands can part the fabric,
like a swimmer's dividing water,
and slip inside.

You will want to know
that she was standing
by an open window in an upstairs bedroom,
motionless, a little wide-eyed,
looking out at the orchard below,
the white dress puddled at her feet
on the wide-board, hardwood floor.

The complexity of women's undergarments
in nineteenth-century America
is not to be waved off,
and I proceeded like a polar explorer
through clips, clasps and moorings,
catches, straps, and whalebone stays,
sailing toward the iceberg of her nakedness.

Later, I wrote in a notebook
it was like riding a swan into the night,
but, of course, I cannot tell you everything –
the way she closed her eyes to the orchard,
how her hair tumbled free of its pins,
how there were sudden dashes
whenever we spoke.

What I can tell you is
it was terribly quiet in Amherst
that Sabbath afternoon,
nothing but a carriage passing the house,
a fly buzzing in a windowpane.

So I could plainly hear her inhale
when I undid the very top
hook-and-eye fastener of her corset

and I could hear her sigh when finally it was unloosed,
the way some readers sigh when they realise
that Hope has feathers,
that reason is a plank,
that life is a loaded gun
that looks right at you with a yellow eye.

Your One Good Dress

**BRENDA
SHAUGHNESSY**

should never be light. That kind of thing feels
like a hundred shiny-headed waifs backlit
and skeletal, approaching. Dripping and in
unison, murmuring, 'We *are* you.'

No. And the red dress (think about it,
redress) is all neckhole. The brown
is a big wet beard with, of course, a backslit.
You're only as sick as your secrets.

There is an argument for the dull-chic,
the dirty olive and the Cinderelly. But those
who exhort it are only part of the conspiracy:
'Shimmer, shmimmer,' they'll say. 'Lush, shmush.'

Do not listen. It's a part of the anti-obvious
movement and it's sheer matricide. Ask your mum.
It would kill her if you were ewe gee el why.
And is it a crime to wonder, am I. In the dark a dare,

Am I now. You put on your Niña, your Pinta, your
Santa María. Make it simple to last your whole
life long. Make it black. Glassy or deep.
Your body is opium and you are its only true smoker.

This black dress is your one good dress.
Bury your children in it. Visit your pokey
hometown friends in it. Go missing for days.
Taking it off never matters. That just wears you down.

This Blueness
Not All Blue

BRIAN HENRY

That is the point where we undid each other.
Unzipped each other, shook each other
onto the snow. That is the point we rescued each other
from the cold, bundled each other into packets to cradle.
That is the point where you promised no more pleading
Tomorrow, tomorrow as you'd done since I'd met you
at the station, under the awning, before the last train arrived.
That is the point I lifted your blue cable sweater
from your body and covered with my hands all I could cover
and tasted all my hands could not hold.
The point where you asked me inside, as I was,
perpendicular beneath the skylight that offered a view
of more dead suns than anyone could count.
As the number of times you asked me inside you that night,
that week, are more than anyone could count.

Oppenheimer's Cup and Saucer

CAROL ANN DUFFY

She asked me to luncheon in fur. Far from
the loud laughter of men, our secret life stirred.

I remember her eyes, the slim rope of her spine.
This is your cup, she whispered, and this mine.

We drank the sweet hot liquid and talked dirty.
As she undressed me, her breasts were a mirror

and there were mirrors in the bed. She said Place
your legs around my neck, that's right. Yes.

First Move

DOROTHY PORTER

I reach past my glass
   take her hand

I didn't plan this

my fingers freeze
on her warm veins

I can't read her eyes

silence

will she?
will she?

   touch me

I'm
right out in the open

I'm a fucking fool

oh jesus Diana

she's turning her hand
moist palm
      into mine

her skin

you could hear my heart
   in Perth

she picks up my hand
I swallow my tongue

she brings my hand
to her mouth

and sucks my ring
     finger

'you're trembling'
she says

my other hand
floats to her

touches her throat

her perfume
her eyes

the hot tip
of her tongue.

Jumping

JAMES LASDUN

He meets you at the zoo. You stand and watch
The mossy, boulder-headed bison hump
Their buttressed tonnage round a patch of dust,
A cayman's eyelid flash its mineral sump,
Flamingos, sea-shell pink, curled up asleep
On cocktail stems of leg, a cheetah pick
The last pink shred of membrane from a bone,
Insect analogies of leaf and stick...
A brochure of solutions – every feature
Fashioned like serrations on a key
To prise existence from a precise world
As far from here as yours is. What you see
Mirrors in wing and tusk, night-eyes, webbed feet,
Your own precise and private arsenal
For getting by – each weapon obsolete.

So you permit him to walk you home,
Assenting as he hovers at the door,
As if assent were all you had to lock
What happens now with what has gone before –
This ice-thin plateau of the present, poised
Like crystal on a juggler's column –
Miracles of balance hold you here,
Tremulous, a stranger in your room
Eyeing the bed, the map pinned on the wall –
He makes a tease of searching for your town –
His fingers brush Alaska, skim the Yukon,
Rockies, *warmer warmer*, plunging down
Nebraska, Oklahoma, *further south*,
Tracking the Mississippi, *hot that's hot*,
Vicksburg, Louisiana, the hot mouth...

Then by and by your moon-lit bodies sprawl
Entangled. You're asleep but not at rest,
Flushed hot and cold, an ember's red-black shimmer,
Your face a frown, twitching on his breast –
Wherever you are you're not here;
That muscle quivering in your hip
Is fear of heights – you're balanced on a ledge,
And miles beneath you, willing you to slip,
Behemoth, Cockatrice, misshapen hybrid
Slavering in shadow; the day's nightmare
Spawn of beast on reptile, bird on fish –
And then you jump, and crashing through the air
Towards you comes the creature of your dream,
Its double head familiar…one is yours,
The other's watching as you wake, and scream.

The Fish

'Rainbow, rainbow, rainbow!'
– E.B.

DERYN REES-JONES

I go to sleep with the taste of you, and this is not the first time
for you are too much with me. And these are your hands,
in the darkness. This is the rough shape of
your face, only. Your hair, your ear, your thigh.
   And then, out of nowhere, your tongue like a hot little fish
a blue fish, glinting electrics,
a fish accustomed to basking, I suppose,
in the clear hot waters of some tropical isle.
Not an ordinary fish, not a fish I could haul from the waters,
                                        or not easily.
Not a fish accustomed to travelling in solitude,
but one used to a rainbow accompaniment,
one used to the sea's depths, and her sulky harbourings.
One used to the rockpools and the undertow, the colour of
                                        the sands.
And, how suddenly you swam into me!
   And was it your mouth, or the memory of your mouth?
Or was it a fish? Whatever it was, it was there.
There in the bloodstream, bruising artery, vein,
as it swam,
heading, no doubt, for the heart.
Then you stopped it,
      for you knew it would have killed me,
and it basked in the blue pools of my elbow, where you
stroked it for a while;
then you asked it to dart, from my hips up my spine,
you asked it to wander to the tilt of my breastbone
where tickled, like a salmon, it leapt
      it leapt;

you asked it to journey from my shoulder to my neck, to that
                                                        soft place
behind my ears
where you solemnly forbade it, asked it instead to
rest for a while, and then turn back,
saying *Fish, fish, my brilliant fish*
            and something I can't
remember now

on the furthermost tip of my tongue, like a dream.

Confessions of an Orgasm

NIN ANDREWS

When I was a mere slip of a thing, Mother taught me that orgasms can't tolerate humans, the scent of sweat mingling with perfume, the sounds of haunting moans. When the time comes for you to enter a body, resist for all you're worth. Like the pilot of a plane circling over a city, looking down at the lights, remain airborne as long as possible, checking out the small lives below. When at last you touch ground, stay for an instant before taking to the air again, laughing as the pathetic people rush for their doors and cry out like abandoned children. No passengers are ever allowed on board.

Me, I love the pungent humans. I cannot resist their call. Like snow in winter, I fall helplessly, slowly, before dissolving into a river at the moment of contact. The loss of myself is always unbearable.

Roughhousing

STEPHEN DOBYNS

Tonight I let loose the weasel of my body
across the plantation of your body,
bird eater, mouse eater scampering across
your pale meadows on sandpaper feet.
Tonight I let my snake lips slide over you.
Tonight my domesticated paws have removed
their gloves and as pink as baby rats
they scurry nimble-footed into your dark parts.
You heave yourself – what is this earthquake?
You cry out – in what jungle does that bird fly?
You grunt – let's make these pink things hurry.
Let's take a whip and make them trot faster.
These lips already torn and bleeding –
let's plunder them. These teeth banging together –
prison bars against prison bars. Who really
is ever set free? Belly and breasts –
my snout roots in your dirt like a pig
rooting for scraps. Arm bones, hip bones –
I'll suck their marrow, then carve a whistle.
Woman, what would you be like seen from the sky?
My little plane sputters and coughs. I scramble
onto the wing. The wind whips across the fuselage.
Who needs a parachute? Wheat fields, a river,
your pastures rush toward me to embrace me.

Bitch Swimming

VICKI FEAVER

You were the one who acted dog:
imprinting me with a smell
stronger than distance,
disaffection; nose and tongue,
and teeth I could never be sure
were playful, centred on rump
and neck; exciting a bitch
in me, who, while I rehearse
reasons why I'm better off
without you, has leapt
over the wall of a garden,
is in at a door, snuffling
up stairs, pushing her slender
delicate nose into a bed,
whimpering, howling,
tugging at sticky,
stained sheets.
                    There's only one way
to lose a scent. I jump into a pool
of unknown depth: surface
among midges, bubbles,
floating feathers –
make us swim for our lives.

Muse

JO SHAPCOTT

When I kiss you in all the folding places
of your body, you make that noise like a dog
dreaming, dreaming of the long runs he makes
in answer to some jolt to his hormones,
running across landfills, running, running
by tips and shorelines from the scent of too much,
but still going with head up and snout
in the air because he loves it all
and has to get away. I have to kiss deeper
and more slowly – your neck, your inner arm,
the neat creases under your toes, the shadow
behind your knee, the white angles of your groin –
until you fall quiet because only then
can I get the damned words to come into my mouth.

Behind Which There Is an Expanse Past the World

TESS GALLAGHER

When it's time to come into her
she says he always turns the light on
because he likes to look at her. Not at, but into.
At the eyes. As if the receiving he wanted
needed to reach beyond the geometry of pursuit, to use
the mind's fixative to close it in, or to be
sure of its sending. But also, she said, she felt it
was his way of actually going further into space
at all points of the body. Because he knew, of course,
that other men didn't have to be most bright so soon.
His gaze was steeple-shaped,

like an embodied triangle, moving out from the eyes
to where he joined her as apex, and into which
both lovers, and lovers before them, had
possibly disappeared, never to be retrieved. Except
once in a while as a child, or as the wish
for a child, the lovemaking carried past volition
into an extension of the triangle's
inner space. And future times into which
the lovers do, in fact, disappear, and leave the triangle
altogether behind, as in that moment when space
reviews its options and means what it's brought
together, the way a rainbow wants to pass

attention on to the imagined, yet unattainable,
treasure, even as its color is avoidance of attention
elsewhere. If the man were making love to
a rainbow he would have to look at it, and
yes, he might. But I am looking with
her man into myself as that lover. That's
the way the triangle is. Suddenly
you're inside. And so is
the world.

'i like my body when it is with your'

E.E. CUMMINGS

i like my body when it is with your
body. It is so quite new a thing.
Muscles better and nerves more.
i like your body. i like what it does,
i like its hows. i like to feel the spine
of your body and its bones, and the trembling
-firm-smooth ness and which i will
again and again and again
kiss, i like kissing this and that of you,
i like,slowly stroking the,shocking fuzz
of your electric fur,and what-is-it comes
over parting flesh.... And eyes big love-crumbs,

and possibly i like the thrill

of under me you so quite new

Sexual Couplets

CRAIG RAINE

Here we are, without our clothes,
excited watering can, one peculiar rose...

My shoe-tree wants to come,
stretch your body where it lies undone...

I am wearing a shiny sou'wester;
you are coxcombed like a jester...

Oh my strangely gutted one,
the fish head needs your flesh around its bone...

We move in anapaestic time and pause,
until my body rhymes with yours...

In the valley of your arse,
all flesh is flesh, all flesh is grass...

One damp acorn on the tweedy sod –
then the broad bean dangles in its pod...

Pentecost

**MICHAEL
DONAGHY**

The neighbours hammered on the walls all night,
Outraged by the noise we made in bed.
Still we kept it up until by first light
We'd said everything that could be said.

Undaunted, we began to mewl and roar
As if desire had stripped itself of words.
Remember when we made those sounds before?
When we built a tower heavenwards
They were our reward for blasphemy.
And then again, two thousand years ago,
We huddled in a room in Galilee
Speaking languages we didn't know,
While amethyst uraeuses of flame
Hissed above us. We recalled the tower
And the tongues. We knew this was the same,
But love had turned the curse into a power.

See? It's something that we've always known:
Though we command the language of desire,
The voice of ecstasy is not our own.
We long to lose ourselves amid the choir
Of the salmon twilight and the mackerel sky,
The very air we take into our lungs,
And the rhododendron's cry.

And when you lick the sweat along my thigh,
Dearest, we renew the gift of tongues.

The Ecstasy of St Saviour's Avenue

(Valentine's Night)

NEIL ROLLINSON

Tonight the tenement smells of oysters
and semen, chocolate and rose petals.
The windows of every flat are open
to cool us, the noise of our limberings
issues from every sash as if the building
was hyperventilating in the cold
February air. We can hear the moans
of the Rossiters, the Hendersons,
the babysitters in number 3; a gentle
pornography rousing us like an aphrodisiac.
For once the house is harmonious, we rock
in our beds; our rhythms hum
in the stone foundations.
                                   We shall have to be careful;
like soldiers who must break step on a bridge.
We stagger our climaxes one by one,
from the basement flat to the attic room,
a pounding of mattresses moves through the house
in a long, multiple, communal orgasm.
The building sighs like a whore house.
We lie in our sheets watching the glow
of the street lights colour the sky; the chimneys
blow their smoke like the mellow exhalations
of post-coital cigarettes.

The Girl Upstairs

SIÂN HUGHES

The girl upstairs wears white lycra shorts
even in winter. 'They're comfy,'
she says. 'What's the problem?'
From the half landing you can hear
the steady scratch of her electric meter.

The corner shop sends messenger boys
up the road with her grocery boxes.
Cling peaches in syrup. Carnation milk.
Baby carrots. Peas. Her freckles
are pale orange under a home made tan.

The landlord says 'She could make it nice,
homely, but she's not the type.'
Her boyfriend laughs. 'When I come home
I don't want gardening and all that crap.
Fornication. That's what a man needs.'

Rhetorical Questions

HUGO WILLIAMS

How do you think I feel
when you make me talk to you
and won't let me stop
till the words turn into a moan?
Do you think I mind
when you put your hand over my mouth
and tell me not to move
so you can 'hear' it happening?

And how do you think I like it
when you tell me what to do
and your mouth opens
and you look straight through me?
Do you think I mind
when the blank expression comes
and you set off alone
down the hall of collapsing columns?

True Love

SHARON OLDS

In the middle of the night, when we get up
after making love, we look at each other in
complete friendship, we know so fully
what the other has been doing. Bound to each other
like mountaineers coming down from a mountain,
bound with the tie of the delivery-room,
we wander down the hall to the bathroom, I can
hardly walk, I wobble through the granular
shadowless air, I know where you are
with my eyes closed, we are bound to each other
with huge invisible threads, our sexes
muted, exhausted, crushed, the whole
body a sex – surely this
is the most blessed time of my life,
our children asleep in their beds, each fate
like a vein of abiding mineral
not discovered yet. I sit
on the toilet in the night, you are somewhere in the room,
I open the window and snow has fallen in a
steep drift, against the pane, I
look up, into it,
a wall of cold crystals, silent
and glistening, I quietly call to you
and you come and hold my hand and I say
I cannot see beyond it, I cannot see beyond it.

One Night When We Paused Half-way

KATE CLANCHY

I saw you naked, gazing past me,
your face drawn tight and narrow
as if straining in harsh sun,

as if standing at some crossroads
surveying faceless fields of wheat.
One hand on the humming motor

counting the strung-out poles from home.

It arrives suddenly and carries us off as usual

MARGE PIERCY

Sometimes in early June I am standing
under the just unpacked green of the oak
when a hot bearish paw suddenly flattens the air:
a warm front marches in palpable as
a shove, a sudden fanfare from the brass.

I am putting dishes away in the cupboard.
You are screwing a bulb into the fixture:
is it the verb, the analogy, the mischievous
child of the limbic brain fitting shards together?
We both think of sex as if a presence

had entered the room, a scent of salt
and hot feathers, a musky tickle
along the spine like arpeggios
galloping down the scale to the bass
that resonates from skull to soles.

The body that has been functioning,
a tidy machine, retracts its armor
of inattention and the skin shimmers
with mouths of light crying let me take
you in, I must be laved in touch.

Now, now. Five minutes later
we are upstairs, the phone out of the wall,
doors locked, clothes tossed like casualties
through three rooms. We are efficient
in our hunger, neat as a sharp-shin stooping.

Half an hour after that we are back,
me at the cupboard, you on the ladder
our clothes rumpled, reeking of secretions
and satisfaction, dazed as if carried
to a height and dropped straight down.

Ecstasy

SHARON OLDS

As we made love for the third day,
cloudy and dark, as we did not stop
but went into it and into it and
did not hesitate and did not hold back we
rose through the air, until we were up above
timber line. The lake lay
icy and silver, the surface shirred,
reflecting nothing. The black rocks
lifted around it into the grainy
sepia air, the patches of snow
brilliant white, and even though we
did not know where we were, we could not
speak the language, we could hardly see, we
did not stop, rising with the black
rocks to the black hills, the black
mountains rising from the hills. Resting
on the crest of the mountains, one huge
cloud with scalloped edges of blazing
evening light, we did not turn back,
we stayed with it, even though we were
far beyond what we knew, we rose
into the grain of the cloud, even though we were
frightened, the air hollow, even though
nothing grew there, even though it is a
place from which no one has ever come back.

Crazy about Her Shrimp

CHARLES SIMIC

We don't even take time
To come up for air.
We keep our mouths full and busy
Eating bread and cheese
And smooching in between.

No sooner have we made love
Than we are back in the kitchen.
While I chop the hot peppers,
She wiggles her ass
And stirs the shrimp on the stove.

How good the wine tastes
That has run red
Out of a laughing mouth!
Down her chin
And onto her naked tits.

'I'm getting fat,' she says,
Turning this way and that way
Before the mirror.
'I'm crazy about her shrimp!'
I shout to the gods above.

White Asparagus

SUJATA BHATT

Who speaks of the strong currents
streaming through the legs, the breasts
of a pregnant woman
in her fourth month?

She's young, this is her first time,
she's slim and the nausea has gone.
Her belly's just starting to get rounder
her breasts itch all day,

and she's surprised that what she wants
is *him*
    inside her again.
Oh come like a horse, she wants to say,
move like a dog, a wolf,
            become a suckling lion-cub –

Come here, and here, and here –
but swim fast and don't stop.

Who speaks of the green coconut uterus
the muscles sliding, a deeper undertow
and the green coconut milk that seals
her well, yet flows so she is wet
from his softest touch?

Who understands the logic
behind this desire?
Who speaks of the rushing tide
            that awakens
her slowly increasing blood – ?

And the hunger
                raw obsessions beginning
with the shape of asparagus:
sun-deprived white and purple-shadow-veined,
she buys three kilos
of the fat ones, thicker than anyone's fingers,
she strokes the silky heads,
some are so jauntily capped...
                even the smell pulls her in –

Fucking

**MICHAEL
HOFMANN**

A zero sum game, our extravagant happiness,
matched or cancelled
by the equal and opposite unhappiness of others,

but who was counting as you came walking from your car,
not off the bus,
early for once, almost violent in your severity,

both of us low on our last, stolen day for a month,
uncertain, rather formal,
a day of headaches, peaches and carbonated water,

by the stone pond whose ice you smashed as a girl...
or how we wound up
jubilant, a seesaw at rest, not one foot on the floor.

Voyeur

RODDY LUMSDEN

I ask her, what's sexy? *Watching*, she says.
But watching what? Four strangers making love?
No. Seeing what you're not supposed to see?

No. Thrilling yourself in a hall of mirrors?
Glimpsing the ocean? Looking over the edge
and knowing just how easy it would be? *No.*

How about watching our awkward shape hauled
into the net at last? The gup of a toad's throat
springing back into place? *No. Just watching.*

How about watching the foreshore folding
and folding its constant hunch of luck?
The lone, long walker reaching home at last?

No. Watching a bass string throb and settle
at the end of the final song? The island ferry
returning late and empty, bumping the jetty?

The long cosh of a thaw? An advancing swarm?
No. Just watching, she says and stares
as the ocean booms beyond the window.

Her tea-green eyes. Her brazen hair.
The malt-musk of Laphroaig about her mouth.
The rutting motion of the rocking chair.

Gloire de Dijon

D.H. LAWRENCE

When she rises in the morning
I linger to watch her;
She spreads the bath-cloth underneath the window
And the sunbeams catch her
Glistening white on the shoulders,
While down her sides the mellow
Golden shadow glows as
She stoops to the sponge, and her swung breasts
Sway like full-blown yellow
Gloire de Dijon roses.

She drips herself with water, and her shoulders
Glisten as silver, they crumple up
Like wet and falling roses, and I listen
For the sluicing of their rain-dishevelled petals.
In the window full of sunlight
Concentrates her golden shadow
Fold on fold, until it glows as
Mellow as the glory roses.

Lovers

(after Andrew Wyeth)

VICKI FEAVER

At dawn, he shakes her awake
and gets her to sit on a stool
by the open window.

He studies the way a white
low-lying sun fastens long shadows
down the bank behind the house

and enters the dark room, touching
her cheek, neck, straggling braids,
breast, arm, thigh, ankle.

A dead leaf blows over the sill
and she catches it in her hand,
holds it out like a child.

He orders her to be still,
then sketches it in – the shrivelled leaf
against her live skin.

Her nipples are rosy and hard.
He can smell the fox stink of her sex.
He'll paint her a few more times –

but always buttoned up to the neck
in a heavy loden coat,
further and further from the house,

deeper and deeper
into the frozen woods,
as if returning her to the wild.

Last Night

SHARON OLDS

The next day, I am almost afraid.
Love? It was more like dragonflies
in the sun, 100 degrees at noon,
the ends of their abdomens stuck together, I
close my eyes when I remember. I hardly
knew myself, like something twisting and
twisting out of a chrysalis,
enormous, without language, all
head, all shut eyes, and the humming
like madness, the way they writhe away,
and do not leave, back, back,
away, back. Did I know you? No kiss,
no tenderness – more like killing, death-grip
holding to life, genitals
like violent hands clasped tight
barely moving, more like being closed
in a great jaw and eaten, and the screaming
I groan to remember it, and when we started
to die, then I refuse to remember,
the way a drunkard forgets. After,
you held my hands extremely hard as my
body moved in shudders like the ferry when its
axle is loosed past engagement, you kept me
sealed exactly against you, our hairlines
wet as the arc of a gateway after
a cloudburst, you secured me in your arms till I slept –
that was love, and we woke in the morning
clasped, fragrant, buoyant, that was
the morning after love.

Near Silk Farm Road

KATY LEDERER

Love me like a vegetable.
Loosen my skin from its sternum,
Knead my breast-bone –
Suckle my gums from their jaw bone.
Kiss my molars
with your crow's thick tongue.

Touch me this morning.
Husk me like bumpy corn
shod in cob –
Leave me
to the dung beetles
and the day-long staccato of grasshopper thighs.

First, I want to make you come in my hand

(FROM *Love, Death, and the Changing of the Seasons*)

MARILYN HACKER

First, I want to make you come in my hand
while I watch you and kiss you, and if you cry,
I'll drink your tears while, with my whole hand, I
hold your drenched loveliness contracting. And
after a breath, I want to make you full
again, and wet. I want to make you come
in my mouth like a storm. No tears now. The sum
of your parts is my whole most beautiful
chart of the constellations – your left breast
in my mouth again. You know you'll have to be
your age. As I lie beside you, cover me
like a gold cloud, hands everywhere, at last
inside me where I trust you, then your tongue
where I need you. I want you to make me come.

O, it is godlike to sit selfpossessed

Ille mi par esse deo videtur

BASIL BUNTING

O, it is godlike to sit selfpossessed
when her chin rises and she turns to smile;
but my tongue thickens, my ears ring,
what I see is hazy.

I tremble. Walls sink in night, voices
unmeaning as wind. She only
a clear note, dazzle of light, fills
furlongs and hours

so that my limbs stir without will, lame,
I a ghost, powerless,
treading air, drowning, sucked
back into dark

unless, rafted on light or music,
drawn into her radiance, I dissolve
when her chin rises and she turns to smile.
O, it is godlike!

Last Gods

GALWAY KINNELL

She sits naked on a boulder
a few yards out in the water.
He stands on the shore,
also naked, picking blueberries.
She calls. He turns. She opens
her legs showing him her great beauty
and smiles, a bow of lips
seeming to tie together
the ends of the earth.
Splashing her image
to pieces, he wades out
and stands before her, sunk
to the anklebones in leaf-mush
and bottom-slime – the intimacy
of the visible world. He puts
a berry in its shirt
of mist into her mouth.
She swallows it. He puts in another.
She swallows it. Over the lake
two swallows whim, juke, jink,
and when one snatches
an insect they both whirl up
and exult. He is swollen
not with ichor but with blood.
She takes him and talks him
more swollen. He kneels, opens
the dark, vertical smile
linking heaven with the underearth
and murmurs her smoothest flesh

more smooth. On top of the boulder
they join. Somewhere
a frog moans, a crow screams.
The hair of their bodies
startles up. At last they call out
in the tongue of the last gods,
who refused to go,
chose death, and shuddered
in joy and shattered in pieces,
bequeathing their cries
into the human throat. Now in the lake
two faces float, looking up
at a great maternal pine whose branches
open out in all directions
explaining everything.

Featherlite

NEIL ROLLINSON

Waste not want not, you say as you
wring the last drops, the way
you'd get the dregs of the Burgundy
out of a wine box. You swallow the lot,
like an epicure, a woman who hasn't drunk
for weeks. I see the tongue curl
in your mouth, your lips sticky and opalescent
as it runs down your throat.
An elixir, that's what you call it,
your multi-mineral and vitamin supplement:
amino acids, glucose, fructose, vitamin B12
(essential for vegetarians), vitamin C,
magnesium, calcium, potassium,
and one third of the recommended
daily dose of zinc. You wipe your chin
with a finger, and put the tip to your tongue.
The taste is acquired; like whisky,
and anchovies, you develop a passion.
It's an aphrodisiac more efficacious
than rhino horn, or Spanish Fly,
it's delicious, you say, as you grab my hair,
and push your salty tongue in my mouth.

Spilt Milk

SARAH MAGUIRE

Two soluble aspirins spore in this glass, their mycelia
fruiting the water, which I twist into milkiness.
The whole world seems to slide into the drain by my window.

It has rained and rained since you left, the streets black
and muscled with water. Out of pain and exhaustion you came
into my mouth, covering my tongue with your good and bitter milk.

Now I find you have cashed that cheque. I imagine you
slipping the paper under steel and glass. I sit here in a circle
of lamplight, studying women of nine hundred years past.

My hand moves into darkness as I write, *The adulterous woman
lost her nose and ears; the man was fined*. I drain the glass.
I still want to return to that hotel room by the station

to hear all night the goods trains coming and leaving.

The Feckless Gypsy

(after Lorca)

LINDA FRANCE

So I took him down to the river
and told him I was a virgin.
It was obvious he was married.
It was the Feast of Magdalena.
I was only doing my job.
The streetlights went off
and the cicadas took over.
At the edge of the town
I touched his pigeon chest
and it sizzled
like plucked feathers.
His leather trousers
crackled in my ears
like a bull's hide
pierced by five spears.
No silver fringing their leaves,
the trees seemed taller.
A sky-line of stray dogs
howled in the distance.

Past the blackberry bushes,
the rushes, the hawthorn,
I carved a hollow for his head
in the sand.
I took off my blouse.
He took off his trousers.
I undid my belt.
He left his watch on.
The cheapest brandy was nothing
to his rancid skin.

He thought the sun
shone out of his arse.
His pelvis played
like a forgetful goldfish
in and out of a fountain.

That night I coasted
down an old road
in a clapped-out banger.
As a lady of the evening
I can't repeat what he said to me:
we have our rules.
All covered in sand and lipstick
I pulled him up from the riverbank.
Fingers of iris
clawed the air.

I acted like the woman I am,
a whore with a heart of gold;
I asked him to give me
whatever was most expensive,
satin the colour of straw.
I wasn't going to touch him again,
because though I wasn't a virgin,
he might as well have been,
that night I took him by the river.

Magnificat

(for Sian, after thirteen years)

MICHÈLE ROBERTS

oh this man
what a meal he made of me
how he chewed and gobbled and sucked

in the end he spat me all out

you arrived on the dot, in the nick
of time, with your red curls flying
I was about to slip down the sink like grease
I nearly collapsed, I almost
wiped myself out like a stain
I called for you, and you came, you voyaged
fierce as a small archangel with swords and breasts
you declared the birth of a new life
in my kitchen there was an annunciation
and I was still, awed by your hair's glory

you commanded me to sing of my redemption

oh my friend, how
you were mother for me, and how
I could let myself lean on you
comfortable as an old cloth, familiar as enamel saucepans
I was a child again, pyjamaed
in winceyette, my hair plaited, and you
listened, you soothed me like cakes and milk
you listened to me for three days, and I poured
it out, I flowed all over you
like wine, like oil, you touched the place where it hurt
at night we slept together in my big bed
your shoulder eased me towards dreams

when we met, I tell you
it was a birthday party, a funeral
it was a holy communion
between women, a Visitation

it was two old she-goats butting
and nuzzling each other in the smelly fold

Song for
a Lady

ANNE SEXTON

On the day of breasts and small hips
the window pocked with bad rain,
rain coming on like a minister,
we coupled, so sane and insane.
We lay like spoons while the sinister
rain dropped like flies on our lips
and our glad eyes and our small hips.

'The room is so cold with rain,' you said
and you, feminine you, with your flower
said novenas to my ankles and elbows.
You are a national product and power.
Oh my swan, my drudge, my dear wooly rose,
even a notary would notarise our bed
as you knead me and I rise like bread.

Girlfriends

(after Verlaine)

**CAROL ANN
DUFFY**

That hot September night, we slept in a single bed,
naked, and on our frail bodies the sweat
cooled and renewed itself. I reached out my arms
and you, hands on my breasts, kissed me. Evening of amber.

Our nightgowns lay on the floor where you fell to your knees
and became ferocious, pressed your head to my stomach,
your mouth to the red gold, the pink shadows; except
I did not see it like this at the time, but arched

my back and squeezed water from the sultry air
with my fists. Also I remember hearing, clearly
but distantly, a siren some streets away – *de*

da de da de da – which mingled with my own
absurd cries, so that I looked up, even then,
to see my fingers counting themselves, dancing.

The Hug

THOM GUNN

It was your birthday, we had drunk and dined
   Half of the night with our old friend
     Who'd showed us in the end
   To a bed I reached in one drunk stride.
     Already I lay snug,
And drowsy with the wine dozed on one side.

I dozed, I slept. My sleep broke on a hug,
     Suddenly, from behind,
In which the full lengths of our bodies pressed:
     Your instep to my heel,
   My shoulder-blades against your chest.
   It was not sex, but I could feel
   The whole strength of your body set,
     Or braced, to mine,
     And locking me to you
   As if we were still twenty-two
   When our grand passion had not yet
     Become familial.
   My quick sleep had deleted all
   Of intervening time and place.
     I only knew
The stay of your secure firm dry embrace.

Past Lives

NIN ANDREWS

No doubt we were lovers in a past life. I remember it now: you were the patrician Frenchman with a sliver of a moustache, and I was your maid, a birdlike woman who ironed your mono-grammed handkerchiefs. We lived on the Brittany coast, and I often walked alone on the beach, thinking only of you. You never sent me roses or dresses or touched my dark skin in public. I wore your gifts of silk lingerie every night and walked on stockinged feet through the dark corridors of a house where your wife continued to sleep long after you had passed away. Often I imagined it was you floating overhead in the sky, not a mere bird or cloud. I still do.

Last night I remembered all this when you were touching my breasts, and when you circled my hips and lifted me up, closer and closer to you, I was listening to the waves and gulls. You cried out as if it were the last time. 'Fuck me hard,' I gasped, wondering if there ever is a last time or a first.

Warming Her Pearls

CAROL ANN DUFFY

Next to my own skin, her pearls. My mistress
bids me wear them, warm them, until evening
when I'll brush her hair. At six, I place them
round her cool, white throat. All day I think of her,

resting in the Yellow Room, contemplating silk
or taffeta, which gown tonight? She fans herself
whilst I work willingly, my slow heat entering
each pearl. Slack on my neck, her rope.

She's beautiful. I dream about her
in my attic bed; picture her dancing
with tall men, puzzled by my faint, persistent scent
beneath her French perfume, her milky stones.

I dust her shoulders with a rabbit's foot,
watch the soft blush seep through her skin
like an indolent sigh. In her looking-glass
my red lips part as though I want to speak.

Full moon. Her carriage brings her home. I see
her every movement in my head…Undressing,
taking off her jewels, her slim hand reaching
for the case, slipping naked into bed, the way

she always does… And I lie here awake,
knowing the pearls are cooling even now
in the room where my mistress sleeps. All night
I feel their absence and I burn.

Troilism

RODDY LUMSDEN

I could mention X, locked naked
in the spare room by two so taken
with each other, they no longer needed him,

or Y who, with an erection in either hand,
said she felt like she was skiing,
or Z who woke in a hotel bed in a maze

of shattered champagne glass
between two hazy girls, his wallet light.
Me? I never tried it, though like many

I thought and thought about it
until a small moon rose above a harvest field,
which was satisfying, in its own way, enough.

Singing to Tony Bennett's Cock

VICTORIA REDEL

Does it really matter, really, if it's true or not,
but just, really, to think of it, Tony Bennett's cock
in his hotel room at the San Juan Americana
while Rosario knelt over it, her mouth brushing over it,
her crooning, 'Ladies and Gentlemen,
here tonight, straight from six sold-out weeks
at the fabulous, the world-famous Atlantic City's Taj Mahal
is the one, the only, Mister Tony Bennett.'
And with that she'd sing, tilting and leaning into
the purpled head, all the old Tony Bennett classics
and for an encore some new songs

she'd make up for him on the spot.
What if it is true, really? What if I told you Rosario is a twin –
would that stretch your belief?
That they dance flamenco in separate cities?
That they are over fifty? That the sister's name means hope?
Are you with me still? Are you really ready to know
that all Tony Bennett wanted was to go down on her,
that she claims that after coming
her mouth goes cold as marble? She has lost me
with this intrusion of marble, and I don't want to lose you.
It's just her claim, after all. I have heard a woman claim
that she didn't like it, a man's mouth on her,
or women who will not take a man in their mouths,
let alone to sing the cock, sing the cock, sing the cock,
and other women, still, exhausted by claims.
I want none of it, I want it all, your castanet heart,
your secrets walking around naked, a rash of honesty,
your raucous coming, not stilled. Does the twin's mouth
marble too? The San Juan Americana, that sounds
good enough to me. And for you, can we say love?
Can we say he went there thirsting her ochre menses
and came up smeary and beyond any backyard Gods.
Tell me, really, Tony, is it true – ochred or purpled
or San Juan? How are the new classics?
In the next suite there is always a man on a phone
claiming, 'I'm just the same in real life.'
In the next to the next room, room service knocks twice.
The hotel charges fifty cents a call. *Can we say love?*
'Is that what you wanted?' he said. Plates and forks,
eggs and meat ransacked on the tray outside the door.
'Not till you went there,' she said. 'Now it's all I want.'

Lovesong
to Captain
James T. Kirk

DERYN REES-JONES

Captain. I never thought we'd come to this,
but things being what they are, being adults,
stardate '94 it's best to make the best of it
and laugh. What's done is done. Perhaps
I'll start to call you Jim or Jamie, James...

No one was more shocked than me when I arrived
(*the lady doth protest*) to find
my bruised and rainy planet disappeared
and me, materialised and reconstructed
on board the Starship Enterprise, all 60s
with my lacquered beehive and my thigh-high
skirt in blue, my Doctor Martens and my jeans
replaced by skin-tight boots
and scratchy blue-black nylons rippling-
up my less-than-perfect calves. Sulu
looked worried. Spock cocked up one eyebrow
enigmatically, branding my existence
perfectly illogical. How nice, I thought. His ears.
Uhura smiled of course, and fiddled
with her hair. *O James*. Truth is
I loved you even as a child...

O slick-black-panted wanderer holding
your belly in, your phaser gun
on stun, and eyes like Conference pears! You're not my type
but I undress you, and we fuck
and I forgive your pancake make-up and mascara,
the darker shadows painted round your eyes.

The lava-lamp goes up and down. We're
a strange unison. Politically
mismatched. Our mutual friend
The Doc takes notes. *Go easy Bones!*
Scotty is beaming and shouts *Energise*,
and all of a sudden you remind me
of my dad, my brother and my mum,
my body rising like a shadow from the past
on top of you. As I press your arms behind your head
I drape my breasts so that you
brush my nipples gently with your lips almost
involuntarily as we boldly go. Come slowly, Captain,
and we do, with both our pairs of eyes tight closed.

Making Love to Marilyn Monroe

PAUL GROVES

He pumps her up, po-faced, his right leg rising
And falling wearisomely. Breasts inflate,
Thighs fatten, force and perseverance raising
A rubber spectre. Plump, comical feet
Swell into being, but her eyes stay dead.
Her crotch arrives; exaggerated, furry.

Five minutes and she's full. Pink. Somewhat odd.
His brother brought her over on the ferry
From Hook of Holland, folded flat beneath
Shirts and trousers. Bought in Amsterdam,
She needed only an awakening breath,
Divine afflatus nurturing the dream

Till it becomes substantial. When she's tight
He plugs her with a stopper, tests for leaks
With an embrace, marvels at each huge teat,
And stands back slightly to admire her looks.
She leans against the sofa at an angle,
Legs amply parted, lips a sullen pout.

Like Mae West she might mutter, 'I'm no angel'
If able to articulate. Her pert
Expression is the only due he'll get
To how she feels. If he but had a wand
He'd *ping* her into life, but all she's got
To offer him is quick relief and wind.

He gets it over with, lights turned down low.
Pneumatic gasps were absent. Self-esteem
Plummets, yet she was an easy lay.
He puts her in the wardrobe till next time.
The sorry fact is real women don't
Fancy him. A shrink would understand.

Who are so inflated that no dent
Disfigures them? Some men need to get stoned
Before they do it; some touch little girls...
At least this shady rigmarole can bring
Release without distress. Contentment gels.
Doubt punctures with a quintessential bang.

Kinky

DENISE DUHAMEL

They decide to exchange heads.
Barbie squeezes the small opening under her chin
over Ken's bulging neck socket. His wide jaw line jostles
atop his girlfriend's body, loosely,
like one of those nodding novelty dogs
destined to gaze from the back windows of cars.
The two dolls chase each other around the orange Country Camper
unsure what they'll do when they're within touching distance.
Ken wants to feel Barbie's toes between his lips,
take off one of her legs and force his whole arm inside her.
With only the vaguest suggestion of genitals,
all the alluring qualities they possess as fashion dolls,
up until now, have done neither of them much good.
But suddenly Barbie is excited looking at her own body
under the weight of Ken's face. He is part circus freak,
part thwarted hermaphrodite. And she is imagining
she is somebody else – maybe somebody middle-class and ordinary,
maybe another teenage model being caught in a scandal.

The night had begun with Barbie getting angry
at finding Ken's blow-up doll, folded and stuffed
under the couch. He was defensive and ashamed, especially about
not having the breath to inflate her. But after a round
of pretend-tears, Barbie and Ken vowed to try
to make their relationship work. With their good memories
as sustaining as good food, they listened to late-night radio
talk shows, one featuring Doctor Ruth. *When all else fails,*
just hold each other, the small sex therapist crooned.
Barbie and Ken, on cue, groped in the dark,
their interchangeable skin glowing, the color of Band-Aids.

Then, they let themselves go – soon Barbie was begging Ken
to try on her spandex miniskirt. She showed him how
to pivote as though he were on a runway. Ken begged
to tie Barbie onto his yellow surfboard and spin her
on the kitchen table until she grew dizzy. *Anything,*
anything, they both said to the other's requests,
their mirrored desires bubbling from the most unlikely places.

Madmen

FLEUR ADCOCK

Odd how the seemingly maddest of men –
sheer loonies, the classically paranoid,
violently possessive about their secrets,
whispered after from corners, terrified
of poison in their coffee, driven frantic
(whether for or against him) by discussion of God,
peculiar, to say the least, about their mothers –
return to their gentle senses in bed.

Suddenly straightforward, they perform
with routine confidence, neither afraid
that their partner will turn and bite their balls off
nor groping under the pillow for a razor-blade;
eccentric only in their conversation,
which rambles on about the meaning of a word
they used in an argument in 1969,
they leave their women grateful, relieved, and bored.

Toilet

HUGO WILLIAMS

I wonder will I speak to the girl
sitting opposite me on this train.
I wonder will my mouth open and say,
'Are you going all the way
to Newcastle?' or 'Can I get you a coffee?'
Or will it simply go 'aaaaah'
as if it had a mind of its own?

Half closing eggshell blue eyes,
she runs her hand through her hair
so that it clings to the carriage cloth,
then slowly frees itself.
She finds a brush and her long fair hair
flies back and forth like an African fly-whisk,
making me feel dizzy.

Suddenly, without warning,
she packs it all away in a rubber band
because I have forgotten to look out
the window for a moment.
A coffee is granted permission
to pass between her lips
and does so eagerly, without fuss.

A tunnel finds us looking out the window
into one another's eyes. She leaves her seat,
but I know that she likes me
because the light saying 'TOILET'
has come on, a sign that she is lifting
her skirt, taking down her pants
and peeing all over my face.

Dear
Virginia
Ironside

POLLY CLARK

I thought my wife and I
enjoyed an excellent sex life,
but recently she informed me
that on the point of orgasm
she feels like smashing up the room
and stamping on the pieces,
she imagines breaking my teeth
and slashing the walls with broken glass,
she feels like a shark in a feeding frenzy,
as if she's drenched in blood
and no one knows her anymore.
It puts her off, she says.
We used to make love all the time,
but now she says she's afraid of something.
She lies awake all night.
Sometimes she even cries.
I want to comfort her.
I almost reach out.
But I'm afraid that if I do
something else will come out,
a deeper fury, even worse,
and I won't know who it belongs to.

He Told Her
He Loved Her

STEPHEN DOBYNS

Party all day, party all night – a man
wakes up on the floor of a friend's kitchen.
It's still dark. He can hear people snoring.
He reaches out and touches long silky hair.
He thinks it's his friend's daughter. Actually,
it's a collie dog. He can't see a thing
without his glasses. He embraces the dog.
Why is the daughter wearing a fur coat?
He gropes around for the daughter's breasts
but can't find them. The dog licks his face.
So that's how it's going to be, is it?
The man licks the collie dog back. He tries
to take off his pants but gets his underwear
caught in the zipper, so they only smooch.
He tells the collie dog about his wife,
how they only make love once a month.
He tells the collie dog about his two sons,
how they have robbed him blind and ruined
the record player. The dog licks his face.
The man tells the collie dog that he loves her.
He decides in the morning he and the daughter
will run away and emigrate to New Zealand.
They will raise sheep and children. Each evening
as the sun sets they will embrace on their
front porch with a deep sense of accomplishment.
He will stop drinking and playing cards.
The man falls asleep with the image of
the little log house clearly before his eyes.
When he wakes in the morning, he finds
the collie dog curled up beside him. You bitch,
he cries, and kicks her out of the kitchen.

He staggers off to find the daughter's bedroom.
Time to leave for New Zealand, my precious.
The daughter screams. The father comes running,
grabs his friend, and throws him out of the house.
Later the father has lunch with a priest.
He describes how this fat old clerk had tried
to rape his daughter. Was it drugs, whiskey,
or general depravity? They both wonder at
the world's approaching collapse. Sometimes
at night the father starts awake as if
he'd missed a step and was suddenly falling.
Where am I? he asks. What am I doing?
The waitress brings them coffee. The father
can't take his eyes off her. He forgets
what he was thinking. She has breasts the size
of his head. He wants to take off his shoes
and run back and forth across her naked body.
Let us leave him with his preoccupation.
Like an airborne camera, the eye of the poem
lifts and lifts until the two men are only
two dark shapes seated at the round table
of an outdoor café. The season is autumn.
The street is full of cars. It is cloudy.
This is the world where Socrates was born;
where Jesse James was shot in the back
as he reached up to straighten a picture;
where a fat old clerk prowls the streets,
staring into the face of every dog he meets,
seeking out the features of his own true love.

The Blindfold

GRETA STODDART

Once in a room in Blackpool we had to make do
with the grubby band that held aside the curtain.
I perched on the edge of the bed while he
tied the knot once then (ouch) twice
sending me in that pretend dark back
to knicker-wetting games of Blind Man's Buff,
arms flailing down a hall of coats,
seeking ever greater dark in cellars,
deep in wardrobes, cornered in the arms of –

In that brief blindness you are bereft
but alert to the senses left to you
like the game-show hopeful conjuring out of his dark
a sofa, fridge, a week in the sun, or the night nurse
at noon, the nose-job patient counting the days
– all that dreaming under wraps! Even the hostage
inhaling oil-smeared cloth maps the cadence
of road and the condemned in his limbo
interprets every sound through the gauze of memory.

But who wouldn't seize the chance left
open by someone's careless hand as I did
that last dirty weekend when I lied to his
how many fingers? but did at least close my eyes
to lend a kind of authenticity to my guess.
And though I usually craved the not knowing
where or how his touch would next alight
now I could peek, like a thief through a letterbox, at him
still faithful to the rules of a game we'd made up

that I'd just dropped and it struck me then that in all
our time together, my tally of infidelities,
this was the closest I'd come to betrayal;
and when my keeper reached forward I flinched
knowing my time had come to confess, naked
as the day, babbling, and dazzled by the light.

Like the Blowing of Birds' Eggs

NEIL ROLLINSON

I crack the shell
on the bedstead and open it
over your stomach. It runs
to your navel and settles there
like the stone of a sharon fruit.

You ask me to gather it up
and pour it over your breast
without breaking the membrane.

It swims in my palm, drools
from the gaps in my fingers, fragrant,
spotted with blood.

It slips down your chest,
moves on your skin like a woman
hurrying in her yellow dress, the long
transparent train dragging behind.

It slides down your belly and into your
pubic hair where you burst
the yolk with a tap of your finger.

It covers your cunt in a shock
of gold. You tell me to eat,
to feel the sticky glair on my tongue.

I lick the folds of your sex, the coarse
damp hairs, the slopes of your arse
until you're clean, and tense as a clock spring.

I touch your spot and something inside you
explodes like the blowing of birds' eggs.

Dear Heart,

SHARON OLDS

How did you know to turn me over,
then, when I couldn't know to take
the moment to turn and start to begin
to finish, I was out there, far ahead
of my body, far ahead of the earth,
ahead of the moon – like someone on the other
side of the moon, stepped off, facing space, I was
floating out there, splayed, facing
away, fucked, fucked, my face,
glistening and distorted, pressed against the inner
caul of the world. I was almost beyond
pleasure, in a region of icy, absolute
sensing, my open mouth and love-slimed
cheeks stretching the membrane the way
the face of the almost born can appear, still
veiled in its casing, just inside
the oval portal, pausing, about
to split its glistering mask – you eased me
back, drew me back into the human
night, you turned me and the howling slowed, and at the
crux of our joining, flower-heads grew
fast-motion against you, swelled and burst without
tearing – ruinless death, each
sepal, each petal, came to the naught
of earth, our portion, in ecstasy, ash
to fire to ash, dust to bloom to dust.

Buggery

DON PATERSON

At round about four months or so
– the time is getting shorter –
I look down as the face below
goes sliding underwater

and though I know it's over with
and she is miles from me
I stay a while to mine the earth
for what was lost at sea

as if the faces of the drowned
might turn up in the harrow:
hold me when I hold you down
and plough the lonely furrow

Missing

ALAN JENKINS

You were quiet, in your bath, and you were going to sleep
                                                    with him.
I knew it, the cat knew it. The bath-water felt it,
and the sliver of soap with which you soaped your quim,
the sponge with which you soaked your breasts, both smelt it –
when you clasped your nose and swiftly ducked
(sink or swim, you witch!) your hair waved like sea-grass,
your thatch, laid flat like tangled seaweed, foam-flecked,
lifted on the swell, and a slither of eel-slick skin
showed like the pearl-pink inside of a shell...
You surfaced, shifted slightly, settled your arse.
I saw it clenching tightly as his fingers gripped,
I saw your sea-anemone open, close as he plunged in.
Looking up, you smiled. I would say you slipped.

*

Missing, believed lost, five feet four-and-a-half
of warm girl, of freckled skin and sulky laugh
and blood on the sheets and ash on the pillow
with the smell of bacon eggs and lubricant – how that lingers –
for breakfast; crumpled things to scoop up from the floor
and press against my face, and cunt-smell on my fingers;
I'll skip the part about love it seems so silly and low
– the aftertaste of afternoons in a strange bed in a stranger's
flat, 'I love the way you go down on me', breathless, 'more.
Harder', and a red dress from the wardrobe, and the dangers:
at 3 a.m. your boot like a bad dream pounding on the door
and the way that anything you wanted could be true,
if you said it was. But not this. Missing. You.

Acknowledgements

The poems in this anthology are reprinted from the following books, all by permission of the publishers listed unless stated otherwise. Thanks are due to all the copyright holders cited below for their kind permission:

Fleur Adcock: *Poems 1960-2000* (Bloodaxe Books, 2000); **Nin Andrews**: *The Book of Orgasms* (Cleveland State University Poetry Center, USA, 2000), by permission of the author and publisher; **Sujata Bhatt**: *Monkey Shadows* (Carcanet Press, 1991); **Basil Bunting**: *Complete Poems* (Bloodaxe Books, 2000).

Maxine Chernoff: *Leap Year Day: New & Selected Poems* (Another Chicago Press, USA, 1990): **Kate Clanchy**: *Slattern* (Chatto, 1995; reissued Picador, 2001), by permission of Macmillan Publishers Ltd; **Polly Clark**: *Kiss* (Bloodaxe Books, 2000); **Billy Collins**: *Taking Off Emily Dickinson's Clothes: Selected Poems* (Picador, 2000), by permission of Macmillan Publishers Ltd; E.E. Cummings: *Complete Poems 1904-1962* (Liveright, 1994), by permission of W.W. Norton & Company, copyright © 1991 by the Trustees for the E.E. Cummings Trust and George James Firmage.

Stephen Dobyns: *Cemetery Nights* (Viking Penguin, USA, 1987; Bloodaxe Books, 1991) and *Velocities: New & Selected Poems* (Penguin Books, USA, 1994; Bloodaxe Books, 1996), by permission of David Higham Associates Ltd; **Michael Donaghy**: *Dances Learned Last Night: Poems 1975-1995* (Picador, 2000), by permission of Macmillan Publishers Ltd; **Carol Ann Duffy**: *Selling Manhattan* (Anvil Press Poetry, 1987), *Standing Female Nude* (Anvil Press Poetry, 1985) and *The Other Country* (Anvil Press Poetry, 1990); **Denise Duhamel**: *Kinky* (Orchises Press, Alexandria, VA, USA, 1997), by permission of the author and publisher.

Vicki Feaver: *The Handless Maiden* (Jonathan Cape, 1994), by permission of the Random House Group Ltd; **Linda France**: *Storyville* (Bloodaxe Books, 1997); **Robert Frost**: *The Poetry of Robert Frost*, ed. Edward Connery Lathem (Jonathan Cape, 1967), by permission of Random House Group Ltd; **Tess Gallagher**: *Portable Kisses* (Bloodaxe Books, 1996); **Paul Groves**: *Menage à Trois* (Seren Books, 1995); **Thom Gunn**: *The Man with Night Sweats* (Faber & Faber, 1992).

Marilyn Hacker: *Love, Death, and the Changing of the Seasons* (W.W. Norton & Company, 1995); **Seamus Heaney**: *Door into the Dark* (Faber & Faber, 1969); **Brian Henry**: 'This Blueness Not All Blue' by permission of the author; **Tracey Herd**: *No Hiding Place* (Bloodaxe Books, 1996); **Michael Hofmann**: *Approximately Nowhere* (Faber & Faber, 2000); **Siân Hughes**: 'The Girl Upstairs' from *Anvil New Poets 3*, ed. Roddy Lumsden & Hamish Ironside (Anvil Press Poetry, 2001), by permission of the author; **Alan Jenkins**: *Harm* (Chatto & Windus, 1994), by permission of the Random House Group Ltd; **Galway Kinnell**: *Selected Poems* (Houghton Mifflin, USA, 2000; Bloodaxe Books, 2001); **James Lasdun**: *A Jump Start* (Secker & Warburg, 1987), by Sheil Land Associates Ltd; **Katy Lederer**: *Winter Sex* (Verse Press, Amherst, MA, USA, 2002), by permission of Abner Stein; **Roddy Lumsden**: *The Book of Love* (Bloodaxe Books, 2000).

Anne McNaughton: 'Balls' from *Exquisite Corpse* (USA, 1988), copyright holder not traced; **Sarah Maguire**: *Spilt Milk* (Secker & Warburg, 1991), by permission of the Random House Group Ltd; **Paul Muldoon**: *Hay* (Faber & Faber, 1998); **Grace Nichols**: *Lazy Thoughts of a Lazy Woman* (Virago Press, 1989).

Sharon Olds: *The Sign of Saturn: Poems 1980-1987* (Secker & Warburg, 1991), *The Wellspring* (Jonathan Cape, 1996) and *Blood, Tin, Straw* (Jonathan Cape, 2000), by permission of the Random House Group Ltd and Alfred A. Knopf, division of Random House, Inc; **Don Paterson**: *God's Gift to Women* (Faber & Faber, 1997); **Marge Piercy**: *Mars and Her Children* (Knopf, New York, 1992), by permission of The Wallace Literary Agency, Inc; **Clare Pollard**: *The Heavy-Petting Zoo* (Bloodaxe Books, 1998); **Dorothy Porter**: *The Monkey's Mask* (Serpent's Tail, 1994).

Craig Raine: *Collected Poems 1978-1998* (Picador, 2000), by permission of Macmillan Publishers Ltd; **Victoria Redel**: 'Singing to Tony Bennett's Cock' from *The KGB Bar Book of Poems*, ed. David Lehman & Star Black (Perennial/HarperCollins, USA, 2000), by permission of the author; **Deryn Rees-Jones**: *The Memory Tray* (Seren Books, 1994) and *Signs Round a Dead Body* (Seren Books, 1998); **Michèle Roberts**: *All the selves I was: new and selected poems* (Virago Press, 1995); **Neil Rollinson**: *A Spillage of Mercury* (Jonathan Cape, 1996), by permission of the author, and *Spanish Fly* (Jonathan Cape, 2000), by permission of the Random House Group Ltd.

Anne Sexton: *Complete Poems*, ed. Maxine Kumin (Mariner Books, USA, 1999), by permission of Sterling Lord Literistic, Inc.; **Jo Shapcott**: *Her Book: Poems 1988-1998* (Faber & Faber, 2000) and *Tender Taxes* (Faber & Faber, 2001); **Brenda Shaughnessy**: *Interior with Sudden Joy* (Farrar, Straus & Giroux, Inc, USA, 1999); **Charles Simic**: *Looking for Trouble* (Faber & Faber, 1997); **Greta Stoddart**: *At Home in the Dark* (Anvil Press Poetry, 2001).

Hugo Williams: *Collected Poems* (Faber & Faber, 2002).

Every effort has been made to trace copyright holders of the poems published in this book. The editor and publisher apologise if any material has been included without permission or without the appropriate acknowledgement, and would be glad to be told of anyone who has not been consulted.

The Book of Orgasms

NIN ANDREWS

An underground cult classic in the States, Nin Andrews' *Book of Orgasms* is a collection of playful prose poems, part human, part divine, leaping from our everyday world to explore the limits of bliss. She maps the imaginary terrain of that upper realm, the place where euphoria endures. Nin Andrews' orgasms are those peak moments taking the form of invisible creatures that wait to lift us up into the air, out of the ordinary and into a place just above our heads, just beyond our fingertips. And yet – curse or blessing – the gravity of our own desire, the weight of our humanness, continually pulls us back from the splendid lightness of euphoria.

'There is no other young writer – at least not on these shores – whose work even remotely resembles that of Nin Andrews. To find her predecessors one has to look to Europe, to the sly and sometimes erotic zaniness of Luis Buñuel. Nin Andrews' *Book of Orgasms* is hilariously Swiftian and eerily surrealist by turns. Talents as original as hers are rare – and are exceedingly welcome.'
– DAVID WOJAHN

'What a swell first book this is – sexy, audacious, funny, inventive. Nin Andrews has a deft comic touch that enhances her lyricism. Her commitment to pleasure is a salutary reminder that amusement contains *muse*. Read this book in bed. I'm sure it will be as good for you as it was for me.' – DAVID LEHMAN

Publication date: Valentine's Day 2003

Staying Alive

**REAL POEMS FOR
UNREAL TIMES**

edited by
NEIL ASTLEY

Staying Alive is an international anthology of 500 life-affirming poems fired by belief in the human and the spiritual at a time when much in the world feels unreal, inhuman and hollow. These are poems of great personal force connecting our aspirations with our humanity, helping us stay alive to the world and stay true to ourselves.

'*Staying Alive* is a blessing of a book. The title says it all. I have long waited for just this kind of setting down of poems. Has there ever been such a passionate anthology? These are poems that hunt you down with the solace of their recognition' – ANNE MICHAELS, *novelist and poet*

'This is a book to make you fall in love with poetry…Go out and buy it for everyone you love' – CHRISTINA PATTERSON, *Independent*

'*Staying Alive* is a book which leaves those who have read or heard a poem from it feeling less alone and more alive…They offer 500 examples of resistance' – JOHN BERGER, *writer*

'*Staying Alive* is a magnificent anthology. The last time I was so excited, engaged and enthralled by a collection of poems was when I first encountered *The Rattle Bag*' – PHILIP PULLMAN, *children's writer*

'These poems, just words, distil the human heart as nothing else' – JANE CAMPION, *film director*

'A vibrant, brilliantly diverse anthology of poems to delight the mind, heart and soul. A book for people who know they love poetry, and for people who think they don't' – HELEN DUNMORE, *novelist and poet*

'Truly startling and powerful poems' – MIA FARROW

The Honey Gatherers

A BOOK OF LOVE POEMS

edited by
MAURA DOOLEY

The Honey Gatherers takes its title from a phrase in Michael Ondaatje's *The Cinnamon Peeler*, a poem which describes the need to be marked, and marked out, by love. The search, the sweetness, the sting and the death of love, are all to be found in this anthology.

Wide-ranging in its inclusiveness, *The Honey Gatherers* celebrates the great passions of John Donne, Christina Rossetti, Shakespeare, Keats, Sir Thomas Wyatt and the beloved Anon, whilst confirming the extraordinary gift to this headlong debate of modern poets. Pablo Neruda, Lorna Goodison, Brian Patten, Adrienne Rich, Tess Gallagher, W.H. Auden, Stevie Smith, Dorothy Parker, John Montague, Thom Gunn, Carol Ann Duffy and Sharon Olds are just some of those who meet in these pages.

Here are poems about romantic love, the ideal of love, the hurt of love, lost or unrequited love and parting – all you might expect to find in such a gathering – but here too are poems of friendship, surprise, celebration and consolation. This is a book which explores Raymond Carver's big question 'And what did you want?' and offers some answers: 'To call myself beloved, to feel myself / beloved on the earth.'

Publication date: Valentine's Day 2003

For a complete catalogue of Bloodaxe poetry titles, please write to: Bloodaxe Books, Highgreen, Tarset, Northumberland NE48 1RP, *or visit our website:* www.bloodaxebooks.com